RE LEASE + BE COME

THE STORY OF 2 SOULS

BARBARA BULLARD

References

MacDonald,D. (2012). Emotional Healing with Essential Oils Manual1:
Introduction, Second Edition.
American Fork, Utah: Enlighten Alternative Healing, LLC

Balboa Press books may be ordered through booksellers or by contacting:

Balboa Press
A Division of Hay House
1663 Liberty Drive
Bloomington, IN 47403
www.balboapress.com
844-682-1282

ISBN: 978-1-9822-3012-8 (sc)
ISBN: 978-1-9822-6034-7 (hb)
ISBN: 978-1-9822-3011-1 (e)

Library of Congress Control Number: 2019908131

Print information available on the last page.

Balboa Press rev. date: 09/15/2020

(c) Release + Become 2019
Designed by Genevieve Jackson & Gina Costa
in collaboration with ContempCo.

Families, Friends and

Communities of the

World of Art and Healing

...Thank you!

Imprint | the art of community

Community is an unfolding of wills merging toward a common goal. It is our intention to facilitate the growth and discovery of each individual that embraces this book. It is our desire to be a pathway toward individual healing. You are the guide and we shall follow, mirroring your experience. With GROWTH comes DISCOVERY... with DISCOVERY comes ENLIGHTENMENT... with ENLIGHTENMENT comes PEACE.

Our mind, body and spirit hold the key.
The Universe will support what we choose...
WHAT YOU FEEL, YOU ATTRACT, AND WHAT YOU IMAGINE, YOU BECOME.

Special Message of Felicitation
Ambassador Anwarul K. Chowdhury

My work took me to the farthest corners of the world. From Sierra Leone to Sri Lanka, from Mongolia to Mauritius, from Paraguay to the Philippines, from Kosovo to Kazakhstan, from Bhutan to the Bahamas to Burkina Faso, I have seen time and again how people – even the humblest and weakest – have contributed to building the culture of peace in their personal lives, in their families, in their communities and in their countries, all of which in turn contribute to global peace.

For more than two decades, my focus has been on advancing the culture of peace. The objective of the culture of peace is to make peace and non-violence a part of our own selves, our individual personalities, indeed of our existence as human beings. In so doing, we will empower ourselves in the quest to achieve inner as well as outer peace. This is the core of the self-transformational dimension of my advocacy around the globe for people of all ages, with special emphasis on women, youth, and children.

Thus internalized, the culture of peace could become the foundation of a new global society. Moreover, in today's world that is so full of negativity, tension, poverty and suffering, the culture of peace can be seen as the essence of a new humanity, a new global civilization based on inner oneness and outer diversity.

We should not isolate peace as something separate or distant. We need to know how to relate to one another without being aggressive, without being violent, without being disrespectful, without neglect, without prejudice. It is important to realize that the absence of peace takes away the opportunities we need to better ourselves, to prepare and empower ourselves, to face the challenges of our lives - individually and collectively.

It is my faith that the values of non-violence, tolerance, and democracy that help the culture of peace flourish will generate the necessary mindset for transitioning from force to reason, from conflict and violence to dialogue and peace. Like Eckhart Tolle, I believe that "the mind is a superb instrument if used rightly. Used wrongly, however, it becomes very destructive."

One soul-stirring inspiration that I have experienced in my work for the culture of peace is that we should never forget that when women — half of the world's seven plus billion people - are marginalized, there is no chance for our world to achieve sustainable peace in the true sense. It is my strong belief that unless women are engaged in advancing the culture of peace at equal levels at all times with men, sustainable peace will continue to elude us.

As it advances, we acquire considerable and long-standing wounds in our souls. Trying to wish these emotional wounds away does not work. Tending to them, on the other hand, will nurture and strengthen our inner selves. We require not only physical healing but all-embracing, holistic, metaphysical healing. Spirituality empowers people to make positive life changes.

The way we perceive the outside world is nothing more than a reflection of our own fears, doubts, frustrations, struggles, sufferings, and the absence of spirituality within us. Negativity makes cherishing and achieving our positive goals extremely difficult. We keep wondering how to be happy in an unhappy environment and soon start believing that it will never be possible.

In the words of Leo Tolstoy, "if you want to be happy, be."
Never underestimate the power of positive thinking.

An oft-quoted saying goes, "an entire sea of water can not sink a ship unless it gets inside the ship." Similarly, the negativity of the world cannot bring you down unless you allow it into you.

Happiness is an attitude. Contrary to what many of us have been led to believe, happiness is a choice, a choice that is made the moment we take responsibility for our own thoughts, beliefs and actions.

Our societies are full of people who cannot stand the idea of being wrong. They always want to be right. Unless we let go of the constant urge to complain and criticize everyone and everything for what is missing in our lives, we cannot truly be happy.

To enjoy living, we should prepare ourselves to live in harmony with those around us, leaving behind all the anguish, conflicts and negativity. This applies not only to us human beings but also to our planet, the only home we have in the Universe.

We are all connected to each other. We need to place faith in the oneness of humanity. We should therefore treat everyone around us with love and respect in the same way we ourselves would like to be treated.

Let me highlight here that by opening ourselves to gratitude for the positive things in life, by being strong enough to forgive the negatives and by not holding on to anger and resentment, we are better equipped to help our lives look up. As Gautama, the Buddha said, "holding on to anger is like grasping a hot coal with the intent of throwing it at someone else - you are the one who gets burned."

When I consider today's tech-savvy world, I always recall the wonderful expression, "the world has plenty of information but not enough inspiration." We have more information than ever but there is a substance deficit – our focus is on material things, not on the inner self. We need to know that it all starts from within.

In this fast-paced and furious world, our inner messiness prompts the perception that the outside is in a mess. The world won't change if we don't change. If we want the world to change, we have to start with ourselves. Mahatma Gandhi's inspirational words, "be the change that you wish to see in the world" are well-known to all.

As has been said repeatedly, life is more about the journey and less about the destination. Change is good. Embrace change; do not resist it.

I have high hopes that the beneficent powers of the Universe will seep into every cell of our human existence. As souls genuinely begin to seek clarity, I believe our disrupted cells will joyfully intertwine themselves back together. If we want to heal, we need to make a conscious choice for that.

I am delighted to learn that *Release + Become* is the first in a series of books exploring the human spirit through visual art. The flavor of this engaging initial publication - featuring Barbara Bullard's inspirational words of physical and spiritual healing and presenting Al Johnson's paintings that explore the depths of consciousness - allows us to savor the "healing powers of art and essential oils to restore the integrity of spirit."

Release + Become models the healing journey of its two creators. I believe this book offers a significant opportunity to stimulate global consciousness and to serve as a stepping-stone into the next realms of human evolution. I am encouraged that this publication will be made available to galleries, holistic centers, and integrative social media campaigns.

I wish the book an enduring popularity.

Outcome

The community is the gel that merges our culture...a culture of balance.
Only when we choose to balance the creative energies of the Divine Feminine
and Divine Masculine will we conquer our most deeply seeded hindrances,
forging toward peace inwardly and outwardly, communally and globally.

Within this framework, let us set the intention to be of Light, healing ourselves
and holding the space for others so that they may choose the journey
of self-healing. It is the new paradigm...the new thought...the new being.
Through the awakened feminine in each one of us, we are bringing forth a new
generation who have the opportunity to balance these energies within them and one
another. To heal themselves and create life powerfully, the masculine within will choose
to honor their feminine energy. Similarly, the feminine within will choose
to balance and heal itself by stepping fully into its power,
living from the heart and engaging their masculine.
Doing so will create a revolution in intimacy and partnership,
magnifying the reflection of our heart's desire. From this place, we become free.
With freedom there is peace.

It is necessary for our Essential Health to Power Up, Empowering the
Mind, Body and Soul. Within this quest, we as Humans
meet our potential, thereby Becoming Anew.

How do we hold this vision and bring about creative cultures of peace?
We must develop a level of intimacy as creative participants with ourselves,
allowing vulnerability, acknowledging our wounds and imbalances. From this
creative center, we can unfold our true desires. Through a genuine and
compassionate inquiry, we can partner with each other in a new way,
reflecting the Light within.

Thus, the inter-connectedness of light is the community. As it disseminates and
expands, as one embraces the light, they pay it forward through thought,
deed and/or simple intention.

Foreword
Nadine L. Berardi

Painting a verbal picture of someone who walks in many dimensions, with the limited language we have, is not something I've taken on lightly. First, let me tell you why I'm trying.

It is only when I first landed in Mumbai, that I finally felt at home and only when I got beneath the skin of Indian life that I learned there was anything meaningful in this world. Once I understood what has motivated Indian society for millennia, I was finally at peace. This was, and is, a singular human society; its treasures and guiding principles elevate my life as I study and teach its ancient scriptures.

When I met Barbara, we fell into step together along the same path, both of us with deep connections to Indian thought and spiritual practice. Her life as an innovative writer, healer, arts promoter, film producer, social activist and spiritual aspirant, reliant on both New York smarts and a full spectrum of yogic experience has embodied the ideals that Indian culture enshrines, in a manner unique to her and to a degree rarely met with in 21st century America. The first Indian yogin to become widely known in America, Paramahamsa Yogananda, might have been gratified to see someone so tuned to his project of integrating the best of east and west.

Yoga philosophy tells us that the physical plane is characterized by duality: nothing is every purely beneficial or harmful, but a chaotic mix that we are endlessly sorting through. Uncertainty is a constant because the flux of opposites leaves every situation indeterminate.

On the yogic path we have the choice of transcendence or integration. The transcendent option is retreat, spending life in a cave, actual or metaphorical, calming mental activity. In the integrative option we remain active in society but we cultivate a quiet mind, detached from the outcome of our actions. Barbara is able to combine these two modes. I have seen her turn on a dime, adjust her facets and go from the deep-trance meditative state of healing, to her work as writer, arts promoter and film producer, becoming cave yogini or karma yogini by turns.

While Barbara's actions in the world are there for all to see, the wordless state of her healing work is difficult to grasp without direct experience. We know her transcendent state only through the results she achieves and the way we are affected. Barbara brings her healing abilities to earth by comprehending and moderating opposites. She directs energy to the extremes of human experience. Her activity as writer and promoter transforms grief through art, as she tempers elation by working for social justice. And then there are times when she is called, unnoticed and unseen, to use her ancestral gifts in direct healing as she walks the city streets, takes the subway or holds a calm space during a gut-wrenching production.

Barbara's gifts are inherited, coming from lineages of powerful healers on both sides of her family. She has been actively healing since the age of four when her abilities were identified and refined by her mother and grandmother. Compassion, along with breadth of vision and a global perspective, was instilled by her family and other early mentors.

However, just knowing Barbara as a third-generation healer does not give us real knowledge of who she is; nor does the deep calm that one feels in her presence necessarily furnish insight into her inner life. It takes purification and egolessness to understand the expansiveness of her natural state. During her healing missions there is intense ambient energy as she becomes a conduit between dimensions, opening portals, clearing large tracts of land or bringing rain to drought stricken forests. Her healing gifts may be described as etheric power tools, enabling her to receive highly detailed information unavailable to the physical senses, to view distantly and to focus light for the removal of obstructing energies.

Barbara's spiritual gifts would be a burden for anyone with less personal strength and integrity; they are so powerful that they can not be taken lightly, especially by her. The clarity of her awareness must be carefully maintained to receive the kind of minute guidance few can hear. It takes a continual release of ego-driven thoughts and feelings and considerable self healing to sustain her projects. It also requires enormous faith.

When I speak of Barbara's faith, I mean a kind of trust unfathomable to most. Trusting that she receives guidance for the good of all, devoid of negative impact, she is often taking actions that appear contrary to everyday logic and are sometimes strikingly counter intuitive. Barbara consequently lives a constant test of her heart's purity, her faith in God, and ancestral and other masters, her ability for relentless work and an almost mandated unconditional generosity, to give and give and give some more. If you ask her, Barbara repeats enthusiastically, "it's proven, the ability of guides, ancestors and other beings of light to influence physical reality; I see it everyday."

Because holistic healing has become a profitable industry, there are now career healers who observe formal protocol but lack depth of experience. Many of the pioneers who devoted their lives and fortunes to advancing our understanding of spiritual progress through healing the imprints of time and trauma on the mind, body and subtle energies, are no longer active.

Barbara is old school in this regard. She is aware that unless we dig deep – get down and dirty (it feels like being covered with muck in the deeper phases of healing) to uncover and move beyond primal guilt, past-life trauma, the anguish of the helpless child and the ambivalences, complexities and ambiguities of the parent-child relationship – most healing modalities are useless. Unless this difficult clearing work is done we will run in circles of endless seeking, taken in by the proliferation of products, workshops, mind/body techniques, meditation practices, diets, technologies and exercise trends, as the gullible consumers of the old wine in every new bottle. We may use tools like affirmations and positive thinking to tidy the surface layers of our persons very much like we apply foundation makeup; and we may repattern our energies like a plastic surgeon does facial structure. But when we rely on superficial remedies, the deep-seated residues we avoid looking at subvert long-term health, fulfillment and spiritual progress.

Like other facets of Barbara's healing work, her use of essential oils proceeds from unusual insight. Her text on essential oils is like her own healing technique – gentle, penetrating and profoundly restful. She uses oils therapeutically, unblocking pathways and allowing light to flow through the continuum of physical, subtle and causal bodies. In a pendulum-like adjustment between the material and subtle, beneficial influences flow back and forth, until they achieve balance. Our collective spiritual unveiling is ever brighter, and finally brings visible change on the ground.

In *Release + Become* Barbara and Al reveal their own journeys through the luminous beauty they create. Their multiple talents open our hearts and minds, nurturing us in communal sharing. We receive their stories of life and healing, are enlivened and become closer to ourselves. If, as the philosophy of yoga maintains, we are all truly one, then shared narratives make that real for us. Classical Indian esthetic thought holds that the space between words in literature and drama is like the space between breaths in meditation. Emotional content is liberating because it reveals our common humanity. Transformed by art, emotions captivate us in a blissful state of savor, an experience often compared to the final goal of yoga.

Nick Dawes

Al Johnson is the real deal. His studio is an extension of a lifelong dedication to creative passion, through art and music, that was not a secure or easy path for a guy like Al to follow. *Release + Become* confirms the deeper awareness Al and Barbara share, that art can be, and should be, a healing instrument. The world needs plenty of healing, and I hope this work will find some of those who need it most.

"The role of the artist is to give visible form to the values of his society, rather than to communicate a personal interpretation of these values. The artist is considered an instrument by which things higher and greater than himself find expression in the forms that he creates. The notion of signing a work of art is of little importance as it is believed that the artist doesn't himself directly imagine the work --he is guided and functions only as the executor. Here we can see the depth of creation."

Shri Sankaran Namboodiripad

The Journey

Life is not a destination. It is a journey.
The efficiency of the journey depends on you.
Magic is there for those who open their doors.
Once you let go, the real journey starts.
The pain from the past can form
blockages but once removed results in
continual enlightenment and peace.

2 is a powerful number.

2 is bigger than 1.
When 2 is 1,
the journey is easier.
Because every 1 needs a 2.

"The school we went to was in a white
neighborhood. We had many friends, but I
was a black guy, she was a black girl.
We were different.

She used to carry heavy stuff with
her all the time. One day I told her,
'if you cannot make it to the 4 pm bus,
I will be there at 5 pm to carry your bags.'
Barbara and I have a holistic
connection."

"I was in an abusive marriage. One morning, my mother
came to me in a dream and woke me to witness a strange man
sent to enter my bedroom with a golf club in hand. I ran toward
the stairs to my children's bedroom but heard a voice,
'he's not after them, he's after you'. Fleeing down two
flights of stairs, I escaped in the rain. Told never to return
by the local police, due to safety…my children, my home,
my life was ripped away!

His name was on the back of a real estate business card.
I thought, is this the Al I knew? It was him. He, indeed,
was still there, helping me carry the heavy load."

"As it advances, life leaves considerable and long standing wounds on our soul. Trying to wish these emotional wounds away does not work. Rather, tending those will nurture and strengthen our inner self. This calls for healing not just in the physical sense of the word, but in an all-embracing, holistic, metaphysical way. Here spirituality empowers people to make positive life changes."

Ambassador Anwarul K. Chowdhury

Healing

Adjective

1. Curing or curative;
prescribed or helping to heal

2. Growing sound; getting well;
mending

Noun

3. The act or process of regaining
health

Healing is a growing process
and we do not remain the same. The beginning
of the process is to have a focus.
Set your intention and let the
Universe conspire
to heal you.

The Act of Healing is an
individualized method with a common theme.
We rise to see the sun, prepare our day by placing the
back packs of what we want, what we need and additional
things we may not want. During the healing process we are
able to trust and look into our back packs, removing
unnecessary items that weigh us down
and drag our steps.

As we become lighter,
we realize that the things that we need
are created by the Earth and readily accessible.
Essential oils help to facilitate that process of letting go
and healing. With our chosen items we are
able to heal and rejuvenate.

"I have high hopes for the
beneficent powers of the Universe
to seep into every cell of our human
existence. As the souls are genuinely
seeking clarity, I believe our disrupted
cells will joyfully intertwine themselves
back together. If we are inclined to heal,
it has to be a conscious choice."

Ambassador Anwarul K. Chowdhury

"You are just energy. That is positive and growing infinitely. The only infinite source of energy in the Universe - is your imagination. Protect it from dark forces, nurture it and let it grow."

"The Universe is dynamic and everything is changing all the time, the lotus flower that grows in the mud, opens petal by petal and becomes a thing of beauty, for a while. Then closes and protects itself from the dark forces of the evening. Much like that, we must let our energy open up and flower, become amazing even as we protect it."

Sonia Manchanda

—————— RE LEASE ——————

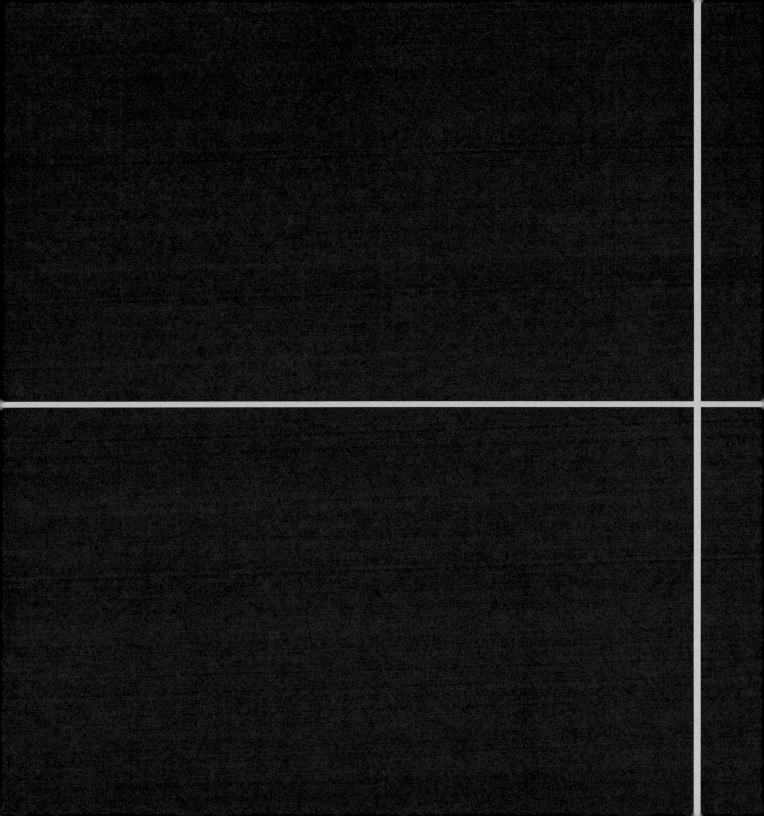

The Magic In You: Finding Love
The vibrant colors of red

Geranium, Marjoram,
Ylang Ylang

In order to find love,
you must first forgive yourself,
then others. These combined oils can
soften the heart, bring a person
more in touch with the
qualities of love, openness
and receptivity.

"The vibration of love
transfers the separable to the
inseparable. As the dance
of love grows in each embrace,
the magic unfolds within."

"The Magic in You", Al Johnson, Oil on Canvas

A Hipster's Need for Chemistry:
Acceleration & Elevation

*Cedarwood, Frankincense,
Helichrysum, Juniper Berry, Melissa,
Myrrh, Roman Chamomile, Sandalwood*

The combination between body
and spirit, Heaven and Earth
has been studied for centuries.
Ascension is a heightened reality
chosen by some on their
spiritual path. These blends can
assist on the spiritual transformation.

"The path for realization is
narrow. The choice is yours."

"A Hipster's Need for Chemistry", Al Johnson, Mixed Media on Canvas

The Healing Sister: Divine Elegance
Leader

Geranium, Ylang Ylang

These oils can support the
development of the Inner Child
in an energetic field of safety,
thereby allowing an opportunity
to trust oneself and others.

"The divine elegance of the
healer moves among us, clearing
the path for others to follow. "

"The Healing Sister", Al Johnson, Mixed Media on Canvas

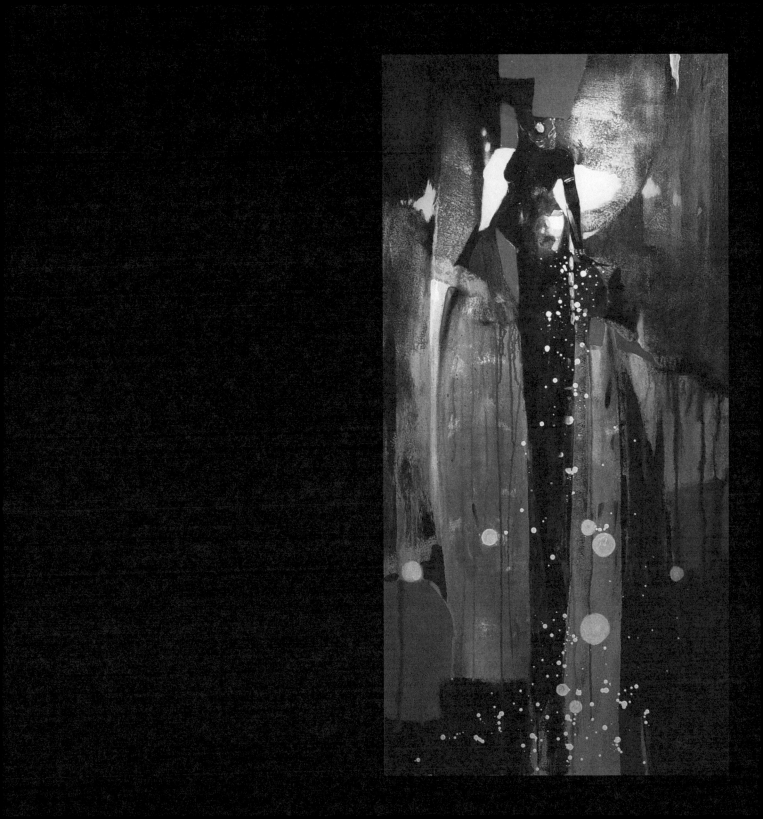

Blue Girl: Moving With Grounding From The Earth & Accomplishing Goals In The Physical

Blue Tansy, Cedarwood, Frankincense, Rosewood, Sandalwood, Spruce, Vetiver, White Fir

These blends remind individuals that to realize their true dreams and desires, they must stay focused on a goal until it is actualized in the physical world.

"Our desires sometimes lead us into the ethereal, not allowing to create what we want in the physical...we must ground ...receiving support from Mother Earth."

"Blue Girl", Al Johnson, Mixed Media on Canvas

Spiritual Recovery:
To Cover Protection

*Eucalyptus, Melaleuca,
On Guard®*

Use of these oils aid in a
protective field around one's
body. At times there are those
that "chord" other individuals
consciously or unconsciously
to unleash heavy energy or to
draw energy from others.

"To cover oneself with all
necessary nutrients of
spiritual growth requires an
ongoing regimen of releasing
and becoming. The cloak of
all things will embrace you
projecting to the future."

"Spiritual Recovery", Al Johnson, Mixed Media on Canvas

Love Permits: The Shedding of Love
Unconditional Love

Geranium, Pine, Rose

These oils help to heal
emotional wounds in the
heart so that love can flow
more freely.

"With Knowingness and Grace,
she relinquishes her love
beyond all physical form for
others to ingest."

"Love Permits", Al Johnson, Mixed Media on Canvas

Laying Low In A Crystal World:
Activation

Clary Sage, Juniper Berry,
Roman Chamomile

High vibration oils with
grounding oils can assist
in the connection between
spirit and body,
Heaven and Earth.

"Joining forces between
Heaven and Earth, the
crystalline structure supports
and provides insight
to the beyond."

"Laying Low in a Crystal World", Al Johnson, Oil on Canvas

Emotion Detector: Security
Protecting The Immune System

*Clove, Melaleuca, On Guard®,
Oregano, Rosemary*

There are physical and
energetic parasites that we
interact with daily. To receive
the support from oils that protect
are extremely helpful.

Immune blends are incredibly
helpful for strengthening the
inner self along with the inner
resolve to stand up for one's
self and live in integrity.

"To walk with Certainty and Grace,
knowing you are not alone is the
essence of an attainable truth."

"Emotion Detector", Al Johnson, Mixed Media on Canvas

Pimpers Paradise: Overcoming Being The Abuser

Elevation®, Lavender, Melissa, Sandalwood

We all have been the abused and the abuser. To move through one's self-hatred of oneself and others, we must shed with support.

"I look in the mirror image of myself, unidentifiable. Somewhere there is myself before myself. The support comes to identify oneself in the abyss."

"Pimpers Paradise", Al Johnson, Mixed Media on Canvas

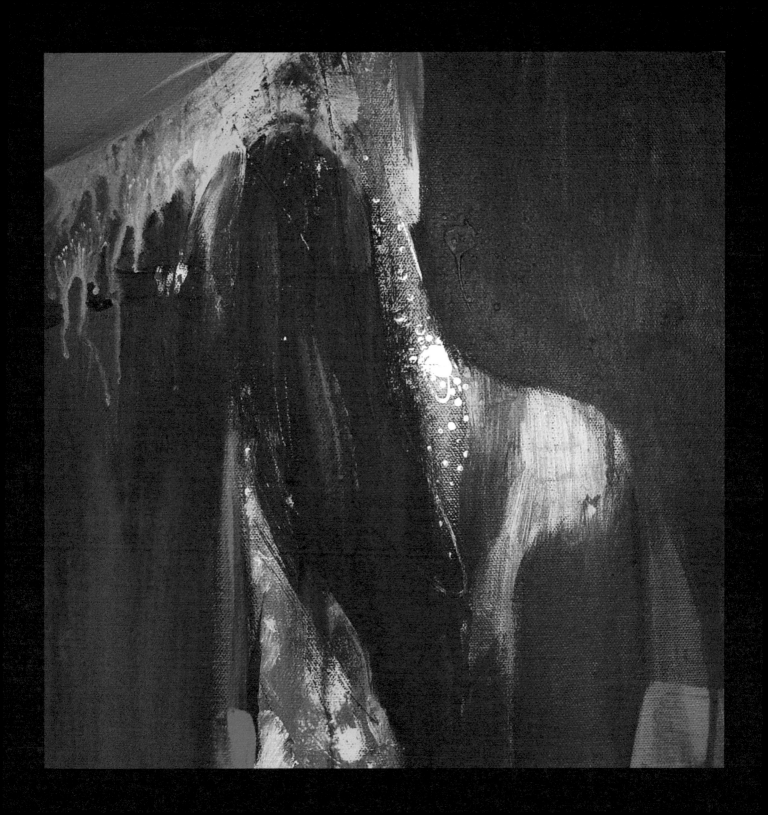

Contemplate: Balance

*Balance®, Frankincense,
Vetiver*

The source for all things
is balance. As we focus
on the center of the breath
we expand.

"Breathe through lungs, heart
and body, from the crown of
your head through and out the
base of your feet. You are
one, in balance."

"Contemplate", Al Johnson, Mixed Media on Canvas

Diver's Deep Dark Secret: Becoming
Moving Toxins

Clove, Geranium,
Grapefruit, Lime,
Nutmeg, Rosemary,
Thyme

A detoxification blend
encourages individuals
to let go of the non-
essentials or anything that
sabotages their purpose.

"As we make choices to
heal, we choose to remove
toxins as we see fit. We are
powerful beings and what
we choose...we will Become."

"Diver's Deep Dark Secret", Al Johnson, Mixed Media on Canvas

Concealed Protagonist
Exactly Just That

Bergamot, Citronella,
Clementine, Grapefruit, Lemon,
Lemongrass, Lime, Mandarin,
Orange, Tangerine, Vanilla Bean

Citrus blends act as a powerful
"fire starter". They return
motivation and drive when
it is lacking. These are
wonderful oils for addressing
lethargy, discouragement,
despondency, or low will to live.
When the soul has lost its
connection to the magic in life,
citrus blends help restore the spark.

"One must move the blockages
within the mind and spirit. Doubt is
an extremely dense energy that
consumes. Releasing doubt will
allow for new energy and creativity
in all forms of existence."

"Concealed Protagonist", Al Johnson, Mixed Media on Canvas

Ancestral Flight: Left Side Flow

*Elevation®, Jasmine,
Lavender, Patchouli*

It teaches that Divine Grace
is for all. It encourages us
to receive support from the
Heavens for more tender
and loving relationships,
providing emotional balance.

"The left side of one's body
is the female energy fluttering
its wings. As mother creates
and supports the Heavens uplift."

"Ancestral Flight", Al Johnson, Mixed Media on Canvas

In Order To Receive: Om

Frankincense, Melissa, Sandalwood

These blends facilitate
quieting the mind,
good medicine
for spiritual growth.

"The sound Om
(phonetically – aum)
is used globally in many
cultures. It is a matrix
of all sounds...the
reverberation of healing."

"In Order To Receive", Al Johnson, Oil on Canvas

Darker than Blue

*Rosewood, Spruce,
White Fir*

Grounding blends
are not in a hurry.
They support bringing
into balance when
excessive thinking,
speaking and spiritual
activity occurs.
Staying present is the goal.

"Looking ahead from the
root of a tree is an amazing
visualization. The root of the
tree knows no fear. It reaches
to the light with patience and
fortitude, blooming into an
array of colors and forms,
accenting the world from
which it comes."

"Darker than Blue", Al Johnson, Mixed Media on Canvas

Funky Side of Heaven: Rebirth

*Frankincense, Helichrysum,
Rose*

Oils can support the process
of transcending from the
darkness to the light,
relinquishing negativity.

"Not acknowledging your own
beauty hides the Gifts that
only you Behold. Allow your
wings to soar in unknown places."

"Funky Side of Heaven", Al Johnson, Mixed Media on Canvas

Give Us This Day: Gratitude
A cup runneth over

*Geranium, Jasmine, Lavender,
Marjoram, Ylang Ylang*

Combining these blends
can soften the heart to allow
the release of resentment in
order for the heart to open
giving thanks.

"Gratitude is one of the highest
vibrations. To be thankful uplifts
and opens your heart center to
receive. Light comes streaming
down from the Heavens to
enlighten and uplift."

"Give Us This Day", Al Johnson, Mixed Media on Canvas

Emergence: The New Face Of Your Future

*Clove, Grapefruit, Lime,
Rosemary, Thyme*

It assists in letting go of limiting
beliefs, behaviors, and lifestyles
to offer space to create and
become anew.

"The cleansing of one's past can
provide a new archetype of peace
and light in all forms."

"Emergence", Al Johnson, Acrylic on Canvas

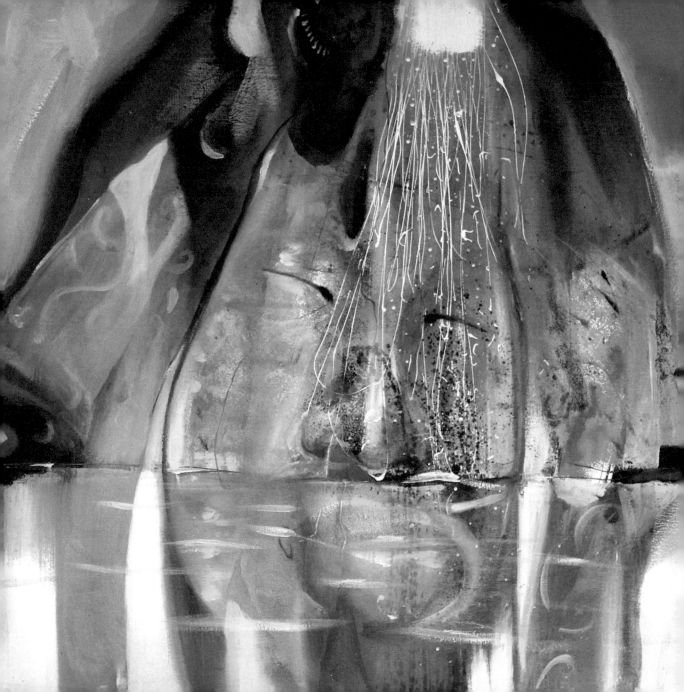

"[peace] should be seen as the essence of a new humanity, a new global civilization based on inner oneness and outer diversity."

Ambassador Anwarul K. Chowdhury

Be part of the community...
Join us on Social Media
@Release_Become

Disclaimer

This book has been designed to provide information to help educate the reader in regard to the subject matter covered. It is sold with the understanding that the publisher and the author are not liable for the misconception and misuse of the information provided. Essential oils are not intended to diagnose, treat, cure or prevent any disease, illness, or injured condition of the body. The information presented herein is in no way intended as a substitute for medical counseling. Anyone suffering from any disease, illness, or injury should consult a qualified health care professional.

The Act of Healing | One Drop

AromaTouch® is a blend which combines CPTG essential oils of basil, cypress, grapefruit, lavender, marjoram and peppermint which relaxes muscles and calms tensions. Apply a drop to the heart area to prepare for healing. Dilute with a carrier oil if desired. For aromatic or topical use.

Balance® is a fabulous blend that balances the energy field. It creates a sense of calm and well-being consisting of blue tansy, frankincense, rosewood and spruce with fractionated coconut oil promoting tranquility and a sense of balance. Apply a drop to the base of feet. Dilute with a carrier oil if desired. For aromatic or topical use.

Bergamot is an essential oil that supports self-worth. Apply a drop over the solar plexus. Dilute with a carrier oil if desired. For aromatic or topical use.

Blue Tansy has a very resonant energy making it a high vibrational oil. It releases the emotions of anger and control and allows more flow in life. It is helpful in balancing negative habits of self-destruction to our body, mind, and spirit. Blue Tansy is an ingredient in doTERRA® 's Balance® blend. A drop to the bottom of the feet. Dilute with a carrier oil if desired. For aromatic or topical use.

Cedarwood helps to ease the feeling of reclusiveness, being left out, being an introvert, the feeling of alienation. Apply a drop on the forehead or rub onto arms and the bottom of the feet. Dilute with a carrier oil if desired. For aromatic or topical use.

Citronella is a common ingredient in citrus blends that addresses lethargy, discouragement, despondency or low will to live. It inspires creativity. Apply a drop to the heart area to prepare for healing. Dilute with a carrier oil if desired. For aromatic or topical use.

Clary Sage helps individuals to restore spiritual clarity and vision, unblocking stifled creativity. Apply a drop to the forehead or behind the ears. Dilute with a carrier oil if desired. For aromatic or topical use.

Clementine is a common ingredient in citrus blends that addresses lethargy, discouragement, despondency or low will to live. It inspires creativity. Apply a drop to the heart area to prepare for healing. Dilute with a carrier oil if desired. For aromatic or topical use.

Clove is helpful in breaking free patterns of abuse, establishing clear boundaries. Apply a drop to the bottom of the feet or over the stomach. Dilute with a carrier oil if desired. For aromatic or topical use.

Elevation® brings a joyous state of being and connects individuals with the vibrations of the Heavens. This doTERRA® blend consists of elemi, lemon myrtle, lavender, melissa, osmanthus, sandalwood, tangerine and ylang ylang. Apply a drop to the crown of the head. For aromatic or topical use.

Eucalyptus is used for dispelling melancholy, reviving the spirit enhancing a positive outlook. Apply a drop to the lungs, chest, and throat. For aromatic or topical use.

Frankincense helps individuals to let go of painful memories, elevates meditation allowing the divine connection. Apply a drop to the pineal gland area. Dilute with a carrier oil if desired. For aromatic or topical use.

Geranium resonates with the heart, providing support for individuals whose heart has been injured. Apply a drop to the heart area. Dilute with a carrier oil if desired. For aromatic or topical use.

Grapefruit supports the body, providing an opportunity for individuals to honor the body. Apply a drop to kidneys or liver area. Dilute with a carrier oil if desired. For aromatic or topical use.

Helichrysum reduces the feeling of fatigue, depression and other forms of emotional distress, bringing balance and harmony. Apply a drop to heart or spine area. Dilute with a carrier oil if desired. For aromatic or topical use.

Jasmine soothes nervous tension, instilling a positive outlook of joy, peace, and self-confidence. Dilute with a carrier oil if desired. For aromatic or topical use.

Juniper Berry supports in obtaining courage to resolve nightmares and fear of the dark. Apply a drop to the forehead or behind the ears. Dilute with a carrier oil if desired. For aromatic or topical use.

Lavender calms fears, resulting in courage, strength, and support for one to speak truth. Apply a drop to the throat area. Dilute with a carrier oil if desired. For aromatic or topical use.

Lemon supports focus. Apply a drop to stomach or forehead area. Dilute with a carrier oil if desired. For aromatic or topical use.

Lemongrass is used to release and cleanse individuals from anger. Apply a drop to feet, liver or kidney area. Dilute with a carrier oil if desired. For aromatic or topical use.

Lime cleanses issues with the heart releasing grief. Apply a drop to the heart center. Dilute with a carrier oil if desired. For aromatic or topical use.

Marjoram helps individuals to connect more deeply with life when feeling aloof and closed off from their center. Apply a drop to the heart center. Dilute with a carrier oil if desired. For aromatic or topical use.

Melaleuca eases mental stress and purifies the mind and body of emotional wounds. Apply a drop to the base of feet. Dilute with a carrier oil if desired. For aromatic or topical use.

Melissa helps to restore clarity to a confused individual. It is also an effective oil for anxious depression and distrust. Apply a drop to the forehead. Dilute with a carrier oil if desired. For aromatic or topical use.

Myrrh supports our connection with Mother Earth. Apply a drop to the heart or on the base of the feet. Dilute with a carrier oil if desired. For aromatic or topical use.

Nutmeg is a common ingredient in detoxification blends that assist during times of detoxing old habits, limiting beliefs or leaving a toxic relationship. Dilute with a carrier oil if desired. For aromatic or topical use.

OnGuard® the blend protects individuals from harmful energies and connections such as codependency, parasitic relationships, or negative group thought. OnGuard® consists of CPTG essential oils of cinnamon combined with clove, eucalyptus, rosemary and wild orange. Apply a drop to the base of the feet. Dilute with a carrier oil if desired. For aromatic or topical use.

Oregano clears away rigidity, willfullness, negative attachments and materialisim. Apply to the base of the feet. Dilute with a carrier oil if desired. For aromatic or topical use.

Patchouli grounds a balancing effect on the emotions while providing excellent mood support. Apply a drop to the base of the feet. Dilute with a carrier oil if desired. For aromatic or topical use.

Pine supports the process of self-acceptance, relinquishing the feelings of guilt, the need to self-punish, self-criticize with the mindset of perfectionism. Apply a drop to the solar plexus. Dilute with a carrier oil if desired. For aromatic or topical use.

Purify® is a blend of CPTG® essential oils of cilantro, citronella, lemon, lime, melaleuca and pine, assisting in protection against negative energies such as psychic attack and negative vibes. Apply a drop to the heart area. Dilute with a carrier oil if desired. For aromatic or topical use.

Roman Chamomile has a calming effect overcoming depression, anxiety, and stress. It promotes a good night's sleep. It can help to remove thoughts of self-doubt. Roman Chamomile is one of the ingredients in doTERRA® 's Serenity® blend. Apply a drop on the forehead. Dilute with a carrier oil if desired. For aromatic or topical use.

Rosemary supports creative energy into action, freeing you from restriction, sluggishness, and mental fatigue. Apply a drop to the chest, neck and head area. Dilute with a carrier oil if desired. For aromatic or topical use.

Rose is an oil that helps to bring balance and harmony with its stimulating and uplifting properties. It is renowned for depression and other forms of emotional distress including post-natal depression. Dilute with a carrier oil if desired. For aromatic or topical use.

Rosewood has been associated with alleviating depression and mixed with other oils can be very effective for releasing abusive memories whether from verbal, mental or physical abuse. Rosewood is an ingredient in Balance® Blend. Apply a drop to the bottom of the feet. Dilute with a carrier oil if desired. For aromatic or topical use.

Sandalwood elevates meditation allowing divine connections. Apply a drop to the crown of the head or forehead. Dilute with a carrier oil if desired. For aromatic or topical use.

Spruce essential oil will release emotional blocks. Spruce is an ingredient in Balance® blend. Apply a drop to the base of the feet. Dilute with a carrier oil if desired. For aromatic or topical use.

Tangerine is an uplifting essential oil that helps to relinquish the feeling of being overburdened by responsibilities. It encourages spontaneity and creativity. Apply a drop to the base of the feet. Dilute with a carrier oil if desired. For aromatic or topical use.

Thyme cleanses feelings of anger and resentment. It restores the wounded heart to its natural state of love and forgiveness. Apply a drop to the base of the feet. Dilute with a carrier oil if desired. For aromatic or topical use.

Vanilla Bean is a common ingredient in citrus blends which assists to relieve lethargy, discouragement, despondency and is also a common ingredient in feminine energy blends that calms tension and irritability. Dilute with a carrier oil if desired. For aromatic or topical use.

Vetiver is known for its calming properties helping with emotional and balance issues. Apply a drop to the base of the feet. Dilute with a carrier oil if desired. For aromatic or topical use.

White Fir addresses generational issues, breaking destructive family patterns. It assists in unearthing negative patterns. Apply a drop to the heart center. Dilute with a carrier oil if desired. For aromatic or topical use.

Wild Orange activates creativity. Apply a drop to the sacral area. Dilute with a carrier oil if desired. For aromatic or topical use.

Ylang Ylang helps to heal relationship wounds. Apply a drop to the heart center. Dilute with a carrier oil if desired. For aromatic or topical use.

*Disclaimer: These essential oils are suggested to be used for aromatic or topical use. I have found in using these oils for myself, one drop is all that I've needed. Test the oils for individualizing your dosage. Dilute with a carrier oil, if desired.

Al Johnson

An accomplished painter and commercial artist, Mr. Johnson has been a professional artist most of his life. In his youth he witnessed the systematic injustice leveled against the wrongly accused when chosen as a courtroom sketch artist for the famous Rubin Hurricane Carter Trial. Through this work he was able to tap into generational trauma experienced on and off the bench, the likes of which drew the attention of national leaders such as Congresswoman Shirley Chisholm.

He was later commissioned to create a 7ft portrait of Chisholm, the first woman to run for the Democratic Party's Presidential nomination. The painting is installed in Brooklyn Borough Hall. His accomplishments include the rendering works of the Georgia Aquarium, which is one of the largest in the world. Mr. Johnson studied at the distinguished Pratt Art Institute, the Art Student's League and also, the prestigious Albert Pale School of Commercial Arts. He is known as a notable African American Expressionist Artist as well as a Commercial Artist, producing work full-time for feature films and television. He created storyboard art for the Academy Award winning film "The Hours" and "The Fountain" to name a few. Mr. Johnson has received invitations to exhibit his work internationally. His unique paintings were displayed and viewed by many at the famous Tokyo Metropolitan Museum in Japan, Susan Bentley Gallery in London and at Maison de Arts in Le Bacares, France.

He values mentoring young creatives. Mr. Johnson is always ready to give a helping hand to artists in the industry, whom he calls his brothers and sisters in art.

Ambassador Anwarul K. Chowdhury

Ambassador Chowdhury's legacy and leadership in advancing the best interests of the global community are boldly imprinted in his pioneering initiative for adoption of the landmark Declaration and Programme of Action on a Culture of Peace by the United Nations General Assembly in 1999. Equally forward-looking was the initiative he took as the President of the UN Security Council in March 2000 that achieved the political and conceptual breakthrough leading to the adoption of the groundbreaking UN Security Council Resolution 1325. This historic resolution recognized the role and contribution of women in the area of peace and security for the first time.

He served as Ambassador and Permanent Representative of Bangladesh to the United Nations in New York from 1996 to 2001 and as the Under-Secretary-General and High Representative of the United Nations from 2002 to 2007 having the responsibility for the world's most vulnerable countries.

Ambassador Chowdhury is a recipient of the U Thant Peace Award, UNESCO Gandhi Gold Medal for Culture of Peace, Spirit of the UN Award, University of Massachusetts Boston Chancellor's Medal for Global Leadership for Peace, 2018 Global Women's Peace Award and IMPACT Leadership 21's Global Summit Frederick Douglass Award honoring men who are champions for women's advancement.

He is the Founder of the Global Movement for The Culture of Peace, a coalition of civil society organizations promoting the culture of peace as envisaged by the United Nations General Assembly in 1999 working in close collaboration with the UN.

Barbara Bullard

Barbara Bullard, entrepreneur, keynote speaker, producer, and writer serves as a social innovator and catalyst for cultural transformation. Her commitment to inspiring through the medium of storytelling manifests by highlighting the legacies of revolutionaries, such as tennis great Arthur Ashe and the first African American Congresswoman, Shirley Chisholm.

The goal throughout Barbara's career has always been in empowering legacy as the living waters so that the story never dies but transforms. Her process illuminates past, present, and future, tapping into the essence of her unique guidance to support the community. Barbara also curates Media and Marginalized Voices on The Hill in collaboration with the Congressional Caucus on Multicultural Media offering opportunities for filmmakers, multi-media artists, and academics to dive into issues and discuss possible solutions of sustainability and inclusion for generations to come.

Her life's work has been mapmaking of revitalized territories such as launching rebranding of performing arts institutions and development of programming for non-governmental organization initiatives at the United Nations.

As a publicist, she has supported leading actors in their unique brands going against standard methods for bold and innovative presentations. In addition, she serves as a consultant on diversity, inclusion, representation, and intersectionality in art and culture for corporate brands.

Barbara's goal is to continue to work in all forms of media producing critically conscious stories for marginalized voices.

As Managing Member of the creative and humanities consulting firm B-Bullard LLC, Barbara supports corporations, nonprofits, artists and cultural institutions in the marketing, digital media and film industry.

Nadine L. Berardi

Nadine L. Berardi grew up in New York City. She left for India at the age of 19, and spent twelve years learning Sanskrit with Pandits. Nadine did her graduate work at the University of Mumbai, the Kuppuswamy Shastri Research Institute in Chennai, and then at Columbia University in New York. After returning to the U.S., she taught Sanskrit at Columbia and Emory Universities. She is a life-long spiritual seeker, who was initiated into the yogic path in India.

Nick Dawes

Auctioneer, author, antiques dealer and decorative arts professional for over 35 years. Considered the country's leading authority on the work of Rene Lalique. Parsons School of Design part-time faculty member since 1984. Previously: Decorative Arts Department Head and Auctioneer, Phillips Fine Art Auctioneers, NYC; Vice President and Auctioneer, Sotheby's, NYC; Adjunct Professor, Bard Graduate Center, NYC. Seen frequently as an appraiser on the PBS television show "Antiques Roadshow" since the first season. Books include "Lalique Glass" (1986), "Majolica" (1989), "Art Deco" (2005) and "Bespoke Mascots" (2014), with international sales over 100,000 copies. Lectures widely at museums nationally. Articles published regularly in numerous publications, including "The Intelligent Collector", "Cigar Aficionado" and "Wine Spectator".

Shri Sankaran Namboodiripad

Shri Sankaran Namboodiripad was born in a brahmin family hailing from Guruvayur in the State of Kerala, India. He was initiated into the priesthood by his father and guru, the late Shri Isawaran Namboodiripad, an authority on tantrika deity consecration and temple architecture, Yajurveda and astrology.

From his father Isawaran Namboodiripad, Sankaran Namboodiripad learned Sanskrit, the classical language used in the performance of daily temple pooja and deity consecration. Sankaran Namboodiripad performs the duties of chief priest in a number of temples, in both hereditary and invitational positions.

Shri Sankaran Namboodiripad took the position as chief priest at Sivananda Val Morin temple, for which his father performed the installation ceremony of the deities. He currently resides at Sivananda Yoga Ranch in New York where he conducts worship and is available for consultation.

Shri Sankaran Namboodiripad is also an accomplished performer of the classical dance drama, Kathakali, an art form which arose in connection with Kerala temple worship.

Sonia Manchanda

Sonia Manchanda is Founding Partner of SPREAD Design + Learning, a new age design firm that integrates disciplines of design with technology and media. She has set up two key projects, The Design Farm, a sustainable mini urban farm where her studio is located in Bengaluru, India and The Design Barn, India's first integrated and independent design centre. Sonia designs ground up strategies for massive scale and impact and leads interdisciplinary teams through tough challenges, demonstrating a high level of thought and craft in branding, experience, and interactions. Her most satisfying and significant achievement is conceptualizing the Dream:In project, an open innovation and design research project that reimagines the role design can play, especially in emerging economies, shifting its focus from people's needs to their dreams, to create inclusive design strategies,empowering people everywhere to dream, believe and realize. Sonia received an award as one of six "Gamechangers" by Metropolis Magazine, USA, and her work has been featured in books such as "Creative Intelligence" by Bruce Nussbaum, "Design Transitions", by Emma Jefferies, Lauren Tan and Joyce Yee and in "Change Ahead" by Carola Verschoor. Sonia has consistently offered her skills as Design Thinker and Lead Designer for corporations, brands, and experiences in retail, hospitality and healthcare.

Meditation

Merging with the Viscera of Art

Vibrations

The Message

Printed in the United States
By Bookmasters